The Busy Teacher's Guide to *Hamlet*

A QUICK GUIDE TO EVERYTHING YOU AND YOUR STUDENTS NEED TO KNOW

Heather Wright

Saugeen Publishing

Kitchener, Ontario

Copyright © 2015 by Heather Wright.

All rights reserved. No part of this publication may be reproduced, distributed or transmitted in any form or by any means, including photocopying, recording, or other electronic or mechanical methods, without the prior written permission of the publisher, except in the case of brief quotations embodied in critical reviews and certain other noncommercial uses permitted by copyright law. For permission requests, write to the publisher, addressed "Attention: Permissions Coordinator," at the address below.

Heather Wright
Kitchener Ontario Canada
http://wrightingwords.com

Book Layout ©2013 BookDesignTemplates.com

Ordering Information:

The Busy Teacher's Guide to *Hamlet* / Heather Wright. —1st ed.

ISBN-13: 978-1515026556
ISBN-10: 1515026558

Contents

The Essentials 10

Context...12

   Chain of Being 12

Format/Genre 14

   Blank Verse, etc. 14

   Dramatic Irony...17

   Aside..17

   Soliloquy 18

Key Themes and Images...19

   Disruption of Natural Order.....................................20

   Revenge Theme 21

   Madness 21

   Corruption and Evil...22

   Tragic Hero..22

Scene-by-Scene...25

   Act 1...26

      Scene 1 26

A ghost comes to visit and the sun rises........26

Scene 2 28

Hamlet and family. 28

Scene 3 31

Polonius says goodbye to Laertes and both Laertes and Polonius talk to Ophelia about Hamlet. 31

Scene 4 32

Hamlet, Marcellus and Horatio meet near midnight to see the ghost. Once again it is cold...32

Scene 5 33

The Ghost Reveals a Murder.........................33

Act 2..35

Scene 1 35

Polonius the spy..35

Scene 2 36

More spies 36

ACT 3 40

Scene 1 40

Spies report and a trap is set..........................40

Scene 2 43

The play's the thing. 43

Scene 3 48

Claudius doesn't pray. Hamlet doesn't kill him.
....48

Scene 4 50

Hamlet visits his mother and Polonius is killed.
....50

Act 4..52

Scene 1 52

Claudius has a plan..................................52

Scene 2 53

R&G don't get an answer. 53

Scene 3 54

Claudius worries, gets insulted, and plots. 54

Scene 4 55

iii

Fortinbras arrives. Hamlet vows to change his ways 55

Scene 5 56

Ophelia is mad. Laertes is angry....................56

Scene 6 57

Horatio reads a letter.......................................57

Scene 7 57

Claudius and Laertes plot Hamlet's death. Ophelia drowns. 57

ACT 5 58

Scene 1 59

Graves, grave diggers, philosophy, and a funeral...59

Scene 2 60

Hamlet arranges the deaths of Rosencrantz and Guildenstern. Hamlet and Laertes duel. Hamlet, Laertes, Gertrude and Claudius die. 60

Journal Prompts for *Hamlet*.................................63

The *Hamlet* Essay.................................67

Topics...67

Essay Organizer 70

Essay Evaluation 73

Online Resources...75

Dedicated to the Teachers!

CHAPTER 1

The Essentials

These are the notes you wish that the previous teacher had left behind—the basics that you need to get on with your job: scene summaries, homework questions, backgrounds to the play and Shakespeare's time, themes and essay topics.

Your teaching time is limited, but you want your students to get as much out of the text as possible in the short time in which you have to teach it. In your wildest dreams, you want them all to love it. At the least, (which isn't a small thing at all) you want them to feel like competent readers with the ability to take on a new text and find the keys to understanding it.

To help you find what you need, this book is organized into 7 sections:

1. Context – Where is the writer coming from? Shakespeare's England and how it affects the content of the play.
2. Key themes and images – What motifs does the writer use to develop the story?

3. Format/Genre – What are some basic rules about the kind of material I am teaching?
4. Scene-by-Scene – What do I need to explain to or bring out of my students as we read through this work? These sections are followed by some handy homework questions that you can assign the students while reading through the play. These questions are also available here for downloading and printing.
5. Topics for Journal Writing – How can I get students to think about a topic or a theme before they start reading? Assigning a journal topic can help. After they've explored an idea on their own, they often bring deeper insights to discussions.
6. The 5-paragraph essay - What essay topics can I assign for this play? Here are a few five-paragraph essay topics that you can use for summative evaluation or for an exam, along with an essay-writing template, a sample essay, and links to evaluation rubrics
7. Online Resources – Where can I find homework questions and answers, essay topics and creative projects for my students?

Context

Chain of Being

In medieval and renaissance times, the world was considered to be complete and unchanging. Politically, socially and in nature, the world was organized in a hierarchy that looked like this.

God
Angels
Humans
Animals
Plants
Minerals

Within each of the above categories, there were also hierarchies. Angels had their own order: Seraphim, Cherubim, Thrones, Dominions, Virtues, Powers, Archangels, Principalities, Angels.

The hierarchy of humans looks like this

King/Queen
Nobility
Middle Class
Lower Class
Peasants

There are three things to remember about this hierarchy.

1) People believed that the rulers were appointed by God.

2) If you were born into a particular level of the hierarchy you were supposed to stay there and not take power away from the person who had the power above you.

3) If there is a serious disturbance to the hierarchy, the natural order will reflect that disturbance by changes in weather and behavior of birds and animals.

You can read more about the Chain of Being here:

http://faculty.grandview.edu/ssnyder/121/121%20great%20chain.htm

CHAPTER 3

Format/Genre

In Renaissance theatre, all the roles were performed by men and boys, which explains why there aren't too many female roles in Shakespeare's plays. In a few of Shakespeare's plays (*Twelfth Night, Merchant of Venice*, for example) the female characters get to dress as young men for part of the play. These roles today are known as 'britches' roles.

Blank Verse, etc.

For the most part, in Shakespeare's plays, the noble characters speak in blank verse and the others speak in prose. Blank verse means that the lines the characters speak are written in iambic pentameter, with 10 beats per line. The ten beats are broken into 5 units or feet, each of which usually has a light beat followed by a heavy one—ta **dum**, ta **dum**, ta **dum**, ta **dum**, ta **dum**.

Rarely do two consecutive lines rhyme, except at the ends of the scenes.

Your students might not think that this all matters much, but it mattered a lot to the Elizabethan audience. They were a very aural society. They could detect the changes in speaking patterns from one character to the next. The plays were presented with very little furniture and no scenery. It was important for the audience to hear the rhyming couplet at the end of the scene so that they could prepare themselves for the new scene that they were going to see next. The chair that a person used as a throne in one scene could be part of a ship in the next or a rock. Since the scenery changed little, the dialogue had to tell the audience what it was supposed to imagine on the stage.

Blank verse also helped the actors. Memorizing poetry is always easier than memorizing prose. There are also clues in the way that the dialogue is written on the page that helps the actors know how to say their lines.

One clue occurs when the beats in the line don't follow the usual pattern. This break in the iambic pentameter rhythm means that the actor has to emphasize words in that line differently that in the lines before or after. It's Shakespeare's way of making sure that a particular word gets the emphasis it should so that it is picked up by the audience.

Another clue in the dialogue that helps actors is in the way the words physically appear on the script. Most of the actors were never given the complete script from which to learn their lines. There were given only their own lines written out along with the line that the person says before it's their turn (their cue), and the line that follows. These short excerpts of scripts were called "sides."

The way that the cue line and their first line is written gives the actors another clue about how to say their lines when they're speaking blank verse. Every compete line in blank verse has 10 beats. If, for example, the cue line has 5 beats and ends part way across the page, and the next character's line starts part way across the page and also has 5 beats, that tells the actor that he shouldn't pause after the previous speaker has finished speaking. He should "pick up the cue" right away. If, however, the cue line has 5 beats and ends part way across the page, but the next line has ten beats, then that means that the actor can take a short pause before he speaks his line to account for the five missing beats.

In Act 1, scene 4, Marcellus and Horatio warn Hamlet not to follow the ghost of his father.

Marcellus: But do not go with it.

Horatio: No, by no means.

Hamlet: It will not speak. Then I will follow it.

Horatio: Do not, my lord.

Hamlet: Why, what should be the fear?

The lines here are spoken with the urgency suitable to this emotional scene with no pauses between the lines.

Polonius who is an expert at persuasion, uses a break in a line to add a dramatic pause to his speech to Claudius and Gertrude in Act 2 scene2 regarding Hamlet's madness.

Polonius: Or, rather say, the cause of this defect,
For this effect defective comes by cause,
Thus it remains, and the remainder thus,
Perpend.
I have a daughter (have while she is mine)

Dramatic Irony

Dramatic irony occurs when the audience knows something that the characters don't. In Act 3 scene 4, Hamlet doesn't kill Claudius while he is praying because he thinks that doing so will send him to heaven. What the audience learns from Claudius is that he wasn't really praying at all. "My words fly up, my thoughts remain below:/Words without thoughts never to heaven go." Hamlet wouldn't have sent Claudius' soul to heaven after all.

Aside

This is a drama technique that doesn't happen a lot in modern theatre, but was very common in Shakespeare's time. In an aside, the actor speaks directly to the audience while there are other people on stage. Melodramas at the turn of the last century used this technique as well, and it was carried through into silent films. An example from *Hamlet* occurs in Act 5 scene 2 when Shakespeare gives Laertes a moment to win the audience's sympathy before he tries to kill Hamlet.

Laertes says to Claudius: My Lord. I'll hit him now.

Claudius: I do not think it.

Laertes (aside): And yet it is almost against my conscience.

Soliloquy

In a soliloquy, the actor is alone on stage. He is not speaking directly to the audience, but rather, thinking out loud about how he feels about a problem in the play. Hamlet has many soliloquies, but his most famous is the "To be, or not to be" soliloquy in Act 3, scene 1.

CHAPTER 4

Key Themes and Images

There are five key themes/images to remember while reading *Hamlet*.

1) Natural Order.
2) Revenge theme
3) Madness
4) Illness and Disease
5) Tragic Hero

Having the students make note of these as they read through the text will help them build a selection of quotes that they can use for essays and projects based on these themes. If they can't write in their texts, students could use colour-coded sticky notes or pieces of paper to mark their texts. In their binders, they can keep separate pages in their notes for each theme and write the scene and line numbers there. Your recording them on chart paper hanging in the room would help, too.

The class could also be broken into 5 groups, one for experts on each theme. You could use the jigsaw method at the end of each act for the experts to share their expertise. The expert groups could also do presentations for the class with handouts containing their key information.

Disruption of Natural Order.

The murder of a ruler and takeover by another nobleman is something that the Elizabethan/Jacobean audience would have taken very seriously. Their own history was full of civil war and dispute with the Wars of the Roses, Henry VIII's quest for an heir, and then surviving the reign of Elizabeth I, who was the focus of many assassination attempts and rebellions. They craved peace.

As soon as the audience is told that King Hamlet was killed by his brother, they know that the story will be marked by episodes of disorder until the rightful king is on the throne. The marriage of a woman to her dead husband's brother was against church law, and one of the arguments Henry VIII gave for having his marriage with Catharine of Aragon annulled. In marrying her, he said he had broken church law and that was why he was being punished by not having a male heir. The audience knew that Claudius and Gertrude would have to pay for their crimes.

Revenge Theme

Two parallel revenge plots exist in the play. Fortinbras wants revenge on Denmark because Hamlet's father killed Fortinbras' father in battle. In defiance of his uncle, Fortinbras raises an army and plans to attack Denmark. Claudius hears what Fortinbras is up to and tells Fortinbras' uncle (the King of Norway) to put a stop to it. Fortinbras' uncle diverts Fortinbras' energy and army by giving them the task of winning back some land that Norway lost to Poland in the past.

Fortinbras' quick actions and readiness to face his enemy are set in contrast to Hamlet who has similar cause for action but takes none. Later on a third vengeful character is introduced in Laertes who wants revenge for his father's murder and begins by rashly attacking the palace. Once again, a spontaneous character is set against Hamlet's thoughtful one.

Madness

In the play, the subject of madness is explored through the characters of Hamlet and Ophelia. Does Hamlet only pretend to be mad or has he become mad? Ophelia's father is murdered, she has no one to comfort her, and she has been forbidden to see the person she loves. These circumstances parallel Hamlet's but she is driven to madness and death, while he appears to stay in control when he needs to be.

Corruption and Evil

This theme is introduced by Marcellus who says, "Something is rotten in the state of Denmark." This theme relates particularly to Claudius. As king, his flaws become the flaws of the nation.

More of these examples will be mentioned in the scene by scene.

Tragic Hero

The tragic hero, based on Aristotle's description, has the following characteristics:

1) The character is of noble birth or has high stature.
2) The character has many good qualities, but also has a tragic flaw. Pride and ambition are popular choices.
3) The hero's flaw affects decisions that he makes.
4) Sometimes the hero realizes what has caused his downfall and reflects on how his life might have been different.

5) The hero's decisions lead to his downfall and death.
6) The audience feels pity and fear at the loss of such a potentially good person.

Hamlet follows this pattern well.

1) He is the prince of Denmark.
2) Hamlet is a loyal son to his father whose death he mourns. Horatio is loyal to him so we know that he is someone who has good friends. The audience likes him, too, because he can be very clever with words and makes jokes.
3) Hamlet's flaw is his indecision. Hamlet delays acting against Claudius right away. Because of this, he has to pretend to be mad, pushes Ophelia away, and kills Polonius. Ophelia goes mad because he man she loves has killed her father and no one will explain what has happened.
4) When he is sent to England, Hamlet sees Fortinbras and reflects on his situation. He is determined to change. "My thoughts be bloody or nothing worth."
5) Hamlet kills Claudius, but, in turn, is killed by Laertes who has died because of his own poison. Gertrude dies as well.
6) The audience may feel pity toward Hamlet because he never had the chance to become king and because of his loss of his father, his

mother and Ophelia. The fear comes from how Hamlet's flaw has resulted in the deaths of so many. Order is restored when Fortinbras takes the crown.

CHAPTER 5

Scene-by-Scene

In this section, I'll be highlighting the key information that your students need to know about the action, characters, and themes as they read through the play. If you have them read the material aloud, it's helpful to give them some ideas of what to listen for (I want you to listen for corruption imagery in this scene. Make sure you note where you see a change in Hamlet's character here. Look for an example of dramatic irony in this scene, etc.) With those cues from you, they will be actively listening to the scene and have a note or two to help them contribute to the discussion that follows.

Act 1

Scene 1

A ghost comes to visit and the sun rises

The scene begins with the changing of the guard outside of Elsinore Castle. Bernardo relieves Francisco of his guard duties and is joined almost right away by Marcellus and Horatio. The opening of the scene contains a lot of short lines that are said very quickly one right after the other creating a sensation of urgency and uneasiness. That atmosphere, plus the cold and the fact that it is late at night add a sense of menace to Horatio's line "What, has this thing appear'd again tonight?" This "thing" is also described as a "dreaded sight" and as an "apparition." The audience is set up for a scene of mystery and danger.

Remember, too, that these plays were performed in daylight, so the description of the weather is important to set the scene for the audience.

Bernardo and Marcellus explain that they have brought the educated Horatio along to see what they have been seeing the past two nights. His knowledge may help them understand the vision they have seen.

When the ghost appears, they state how much the ghost looks like the late king and encourage Horatio to speak to it. He tries but the ghost disappears.

Horatio is afraid that the ghost is predicting some dangers to Denmark "some strange eruption to our state."

Marcellus wants to know why the country appears to be getting ready for war—building canons, making ships—and Horatio explains that Fortinbras, the son of the late King of Norway, has raised an army and wants revenge on Denmark, because its King, who is now also dead, was responsible for his father's death. Horatio talks a bout ancient Rome and says that the appearance of ghosts is a bad omen. The ghost appears again, and disappears when the rooster crows. Marcellus explains that the roosters crow all night at Christmas so that the night Christ was born won't be spoiled by the evil of walking spirits.

At the end of the scene, they decide to tell Hamlet that they have seen his father's ghost.

Questions

1. Describe the prevailing atmosphere in this scene. Explain how this atmosphere is created.
2. Horatio is introduced as a scholar. How does Shakespeare reveal this characteristic?
3. What reasons does Horatio give that might explain the appearance of the ghost?
4. List any references to corruption in this scene.

Scene 2

Hamlet and family.

The scene opens with a speech from the king, Claudius that explains to the audience what is happening in the kingdom of Denmark. First he talks about the country's sorrow to have lost their king and the joy that his brother has married the dead king's wife. Claudius shows himself to be a diplomat here reminding his listeners that he got their advice first before marrying, and that he was just doing what was best for the country.

Second, he talks about the threat of Fortinbras. Fortinbras intends to attack a country that he thinks is week because of the king's death "thinking by our late dear brother's death/our state to be disjoint, and out of frame." Claudius has written to Fortinbras' uncle, the King of Norway, telling him to stop Fortinbras from attaching Denmark. He sends Cornelius and Voltimand with the message.

Third, he addresses Laertes who wants to leave Denmark and go back to university in France. The king defers to Laertes' father Polonius. We learn that Polonius is a valued adviser to the king. Polonius agrees that Laertes must leave, so the king gives his consent.

Finally, he addresses his nephew, Hamlet, calling him "my cousin, Hamlet, and my son."

Hamlet replies with an aside to the audience with a line that implies he is less than happy to be called this man's son, so we know right away that there is conflict. The king wants Hamlet to change from his mourning clothes and so does the queen. She tells him that every living thing dies, and wonders why this death is so special that he remains in mourning longer than everyone else. Hamlet replies, telling her that he is not wearing black to appear sad, but that he is truly sad and grieving on the inside as well.

Claudius tries to talk him out of it saying that his show of sorrow is stubbornness, and unmanly, and a fault against heaven. He promises Hamlet the throne after he dies and asks him to stay at court rather than go back to university. His mother asks him to stay, too, and he agrees.

Once the room clears and Hamlet is left alone, we find out why he is so angry. We find out that he wishes her were dead and has considered suicide ("self-slaughter") He compares the world to an unweeded garden overgrown with only plants that are rotting.

His father was only dead a month before his mother married his brother. This would be against church law and the Elizabethans would know all about it, because Henry VIII needed special approval from the Pope to marry his brother's wife, Catherine of Aragon, after his brother died, otherwise such a marriage would be considered sinful (Hamlet's later reference to "incestuous sheets".). Hamlet is disgusted with his mother who has traded a worthy man for an unworthy one. ("Hyperion to a satyr.")

Horatio and Marcellus arrive, and Hamlet is happy to see his friend from university.

Hamlet makes a joke at the expense of Denmark's reputation as a country of drinkers. "We'll teach you to drink, ere you depart." "No jocund health that Denmark drinks today, But the great cannon to the clouds shall tell," This is not the way he wants his country to be thought of.

Horatio tells Hamlet what he was told by Marcellus and Bernardo and also what he, himself, saw the night before. Hamlet decides to join them between 11 and 12 that night. He is afraid that the appearance of the ghost means that "all is not well" and he suspects "some foul play."

Questions

1. What qualities of Hamlet's character are brought out by
    a. his first words in the play
    b. what he says in his soliloquy
    c. his conversation with Horatio and the sentries?
2. Outline the Norwegian situation as presented in this scene.

3. Find any references to corruption in this scene.
4. Why is Hamlet angry at Claudius and Gertrude?

Scene 3

Polonius says goodbye to Laertes and both Laertes and Polonius talk to Ophelia about Hamlet.

Laertes and Ophelia seem to be very close. He asks for her to write to him right away. He warns her that Hamlet can't be trusted. Though he appears to be fond of Ophelia, Hamlet can't make his own decisions about whom he can marry because he is going to be king. Laertes doesn't want Ophelia to lose her virtue to Hamlet.

She agrees to be careful but teases Laertes that he shouldn't tell her to keep pure, if he plans to go out and do the opposite himself "Do not … Show me the steep and thorny way to heaven, Whiles like a puff'd and reckless libertine, himself the primrose path of dalliance treads."

Polonius takes a long time to say good-bye to Laertes, leaving him with a lot of advice about how to survive in the world and protect his good name. He appears to be a conscientious father concerned about his children

Once Laertes leaves, Polonius talks to Ophelia about Hamlet, also urging her to not be naïve and believe that he is in love with her, but rather to understand that Hamlet is just saying he loves her in order to get her into bed. Polonius tells her to stop talking to Hamlet. She agrees to obey her father.

Questions

1. How does Laertes' advice to Ophelia resemble a) Polonius' advice to Laertes? B) Polonius' advice to Ophelia?
2. How is sympathy created in this scene for a) Ophelia, b) Hamlet?
3. What do you think of Polonius' advice to Laertes? Is it good advice or not? Explain your answer.

Scene 4

Hamlet, Marcellus and Horatio meet near midnight to see the ghost. Once again it is cold.

The cannons are being fired to announce that the king is drinking. Hamlet is ashamed of this. He thinks that Denmark has a bad reputation for being home to "drunkards" and the king's behavior doesn't help.

In lines 23 to 38, Hamlet explains that he believes that some men are born with a flaw, and that, no matter what kind of life they lead, this flaw will eventually corrupt the person and lead to scandal. No matter what a person does, he or she cannot escape this destiny no matter if they are "as pure as grace."

The ghost enters and Hamlet is determined to speak to it. He wants to know why it has left the grave to find other men. The ghost signals for Hamlet to follow him. Horatio is afraid that the ghost will lead Hamlet to madness. Hamlet refuses to be held back and follows the ghost. The others decide to follow him.

Questions

1. Why is Hamlet embarrassed by Claudius' behavior this night?
2. What is Hamlet's theory about the flaws people are born with? Do you agree with his theory? Explain why or why not.

Scene 5

The Ghost Reveals a Murder

The Ghost tells Hamlet that he is, indeed, his father's ghost and that he has been murdered by his own brother while sleeping in his orchard. Hamlet's line, "O my prophetic soul! My uncle?" reveals that he has suspected murder from the beginning.

The Ghost calls Claudius "incestuous" and "adulterous". Church law forbad the marriage of a wife to a husband's dead brother, so Claudius and Gertrude are committing a sin by marrying. The word "adulterous" hints that Gertrude and Claudius were lovers before Hamlet's father was murdered. The ghost's description of Gertrude as a "seeming-virtuous queen" also reinforces this suspicion.

The Ghost describes his horrible death and explains that he is cursed because he died without having confessed his sins. He encourages Hamlet to revenge his death, but not to punish his mother "Leave her to heaven." The ghost leaves as dawn is coming.

Hamlet swears to revenge his father's death and then he is interrupted by Horatio and Marcellus. In his conversation with them, it's clear that Hamlet is still distracted by what has just happened and he makes the two men swear that they won't speak of what they saw. Hamlet hears the ghost but the others do not this time.

Questions

1. What does the ghost tell Hamlet about his death?
2. What does Hamlet's line, "O my prophetic soul" tell us about what Hamlet suspected?

3. Why does the ghost tell Hamlet not to punish Gertrude?
4. What does Hamlet make the men do before they leave? Why?

Act 2

Scene 1

Polonius the spy

The first part of this scene is often cut, but it reveals an important characteristic of Polonius' character. He hires a spy to find out what Laertes is doing in Paris. He instructs Reynaldo to say unflattering things about Laertes to see if they are denied by his friends. "By indirections find directions out." This aspect of Polonius' character prepares us for his willingness to set up his daughter in a trap for Hamlet so that he and Claudius can spy on them to find out the cause of Hamlet's madness.

In the second half of the scene, Ophelia enters. She has been frightened by Hamlet and comes to tell her father what happened. She assures her father that she had done what he told her to do with regard to Hamlet, and "did repel his letters, and denied/His access to me." Polonius decides that her refusals of Hamlet have made

him mad and he takes Ophelia to tell the king about
Hamlet's behavior.

Questions

1. What do we learn about Polonius' character in his conversation with Reynaldo?
2. Why is Ophelia so upset?
3. What conclusion does Polonius draw from the description of Hamlet's behavior? What does he decide to do next?

Scene 2

More spies

Rosencrantz and Guildenstern, Hamlet's friends from university, arrive in court. They have been asked there by Claudius and Gertrude to cheer up Hamlet and to find out the cause of his strange behavior and report back what they have learned.

Voltimand and Cornelius return from Norway with news about Fortinbras. The King of Norway has stopped Fortinbras' plans to attack Denmark. He has given Fortinbras 3000 crowns a year and told him to take his arm to attach the Poles. He has also asked Claudius to allow Fortinbras to cross Denmark in peace on his way to attack Poland. Claudius is pleased at the result.

Polonius brings up the topic of Hamlet's madness. He reads a letter that Hamlet wrote to Ophelia and tells Gertrude and Claudius that Hamlet has gone mad because Polonius stopped his daughter from having anything to do with Hamlet. Claudius wants to be sure. "How can we try it further?" And Polonius decides to "let loose my daughter" in a place where Hamlet usually walks every day. Polonius and Claudius will hide behind a curtain and watch them meet. The way Hamlet reacts to Ophelia will prove that she is the cause of his madness.

After Polonius is left alone, Hamlet enters reading a book and Polonius decides to talk to him. Hamlet spends a lot of this scene insulting Polonius. Polonius is clever enough to say, "Tough this be madness, yet there is method in't" suspecting that Hamlet, though mad, still has some of his wits about him.

Hamlet is clearly very sad when he says "You cannot take from me anything that I will more willingly part withal: except my life, except my life, except my life."

Once Polonius leaves, Rosencrantz and Guildenstern arrive and Hamlet seems genuinely happy to see his two old friends. They happily play with words, something that Hamlet enjoys and that was clearly part of their relationship when at university.

Soon Hamlet is suspicious as to why they are there and makes them admit that they were "sent for." Hamlet admits that he has behaved strangely lately and reveals that he is not delighted by anyone's company "man delights not me, nor woman neither."

Rosencrantz and Guildenstern tell him that the players are coming to perform at the castle. Shakespeare takes this opportunity to make comments about the state of theatre in London at that time and the new fad of children putting on plays.

Before Polonius returns, Hamlet hints that his madness his affected by the wind—that he's not mad all the time and knows who is a friend and who is not. "I am mad north-north-west: when the wind is southerly I know a hawk from a handsaw." This is a warning to Rosencrantz and Guildenstern, but they choose to ignore it through their actions later.

Once again, Hamlet has fun at Polonius' expense. Hamlet is happy to see the Players whom he seems to know well and he asks them to perform a recitation right away. He shows his own ability to recite before the First Player takes over. Polonius is easily bored and thinks the speech is too long, and is later surprised at the effect the speech has on the actor performing it. Hamlet scolds Polonius for his comment about giving the players accommodations that suit their station in life. Hamlet encourages him to "use every man after his desert, and who shall 'scape whipping? Use them after your own honor and dignity; the less they deserve, the more merit is in your bounty."

Hamlet asks the First Player to perform the play called *The Murder of Gonzago* and to add a speech to it that he will write and give to the actor to perform. The First Player agrees.

The First Player's performance makes Hamlet reflect on his inaction in the revenge of his father's murder. He is ashamed that the Frist Player can experience such profound emotions over a fictional character, and yet he can't stir himself over something as important has is father's death. Hamlet is angry and calls himself a coward, and compares himself to a woman screaming in the streets, making a lot of noise but doing nothing. At the time, all ghosts were thought to be evil. What if this ghost is evil, too, and plotting his downfall? Hamlet explains his plan to have the players perform a play that reenacts the murder of his father. He'll watch Claudius' reaction and know for himself that Claudius is really guilty. Hamlet hints at his own "melancholy." His preoccupation with wanting to rid himself of "my life," his deep mourning at the beginning of the play would make a look at his character and his strange behavior in terms of clinical depression and interesting project for students to investigate.

Questions

1. Why have Rosencrantz and Guildenstern been summoned to meet with Claudius and Gertrude?
2. What news has Claudius heard from Norway?
3. What reason does Polonius suggest is the cause of Hamlet's strange behavior?
4. What plan is devised to prove or disprove Polonius' theory about Hamlet?

ACT 3

Scene 1

Spies report and a trap is set.

The scene opens with Rosencrantz and Guildenstern passing along their opinions of Hamlet to Claudius and Gertrude, along with Hamlet's wish that Claudius and Gertrude attend the play. When Rosencrantz and Guildenstern leave, Claudius explains to Gertrude that he and Polonius are going to spy on Hamlet as he meets Ophelia and see if the cause of his madness is really his love for Ophelia that she has refused to return.

Polonius tells Ophelia to read a book to explain while she is alone and makes a reference to how a look of devotion can hide a devil. This comment hits home to Claudius "How smart a lash that speech doth give my conscience!" because he is hiding the crime that he has committed "O heavy burden!"

Next comes the most well-known of Hamlet's soliloquies, and once again, we see him playing with the idea of ending his life. Initially death seems like a peaceful thing, like sleeping, compared to how difficult it is to live with problems and the weakness of the body.

Then he wonders what will happen if that sleep is full of dreams, or a worse place to be than alive in the world. No one would willingly suffer if he didn't fear even more what would happen after death. "… that dread of something after death,/The undiscover'd country, from whose bourn/No traveler returns." Fearing the unknown makes people stay and suffer on earth because they have a greater fear of what will happen after death. "Thus conscience doth make cowards of us all."

This soliloquy tells us once again how sad and helpless that Hamlet feels. It also shows his intelligence that he can argue on both sides of the decision to "shuffle off this mortal coil." He might be thinking about his father and what he is suffering after his death. We also see his tendency to think through all of his decisions. He thoroughly considers all the options to an easy death. This characteristic of thinking about his actions sometimes causes him to not act at all.

At the end of the soliloquy, Hamlet sees Ophelia. She tries to return the gifts he gave her earlier, and when he refuses them, she reminds him with how much affection he originally gave them to her and asks him again to take them from her.

At this point, Hamlet seems to go on the attack. In most productions, it is at this point that Hamlet notices, because of a noise or a movement from behind a curtain, that they are being watched. He scolds her for not being as honest as her good looks imply that she should be. He tells her that he loved her once and then says that she should have not believed him and that he doesn't love her. Knowing what he is going to do (kill his uncle,) he may be trying to distance her from him to protect her.

Hamlet tells Ophelia to go to a nunnery so that she will not be near him anymore as he has many faults and could hurt her. When she lies about where her father is, Hamlet turns on her and curses her "I'll give thee this plague for thy dowry" that not matter what she does she won't escape slander (calumny) perhaps from being associated with him and what he has become being mad and what he will become a murderer of his uncle. Hamlet's rage against women in his last speech before he exits is as much against Ophelia as it is against his mother.

Ophelia is distraught at the madness she has seen in Hamlet "a great mind is here o'erthrown" and is "wretched" because she loved him once and believed he loved her. The change in this Hamlet from the Hamlet she loved causes her deep sorrow "O, woe is me,/To have seen what I have seen, see what I see!"

Claudius is not convinced that Hamlet's madness is caused by rejected love. He plans to send Hamlet to England as soon as possible, saying that he hopes that travel will help cure his madness. Polonius is still convinced that "neglected love" is the cause, and suggests that Gertrude speak to Hamlet and see if she can find out the truth. He will listen to the conversation. He encourages Claudius to postpone sending Hamlet away, until Polonius has watched Hamlet talk to his mother.

Questions

1. In his soliloquy, what reason does Hamlet give to explain why people who are suffering don't end their lives?
2. At what point in his conversation with Ophelia, does Hamlet become aware that they are being watched? Compare his behavior before and after that moment.
3. After witnessing the scene between Hamlet and Ophelia, is Claudius convinced that Hamlet's sadness/madness is caused by his relationship with Ophelia?
4. What is Polonius' next plan to get to the root of Hamlet's problem?

Scene 2

The play's the thing.

The scene begins with Hamlet's famous advice to the players. It's clear that Shakespeare has a particular acting style in mind for the success of his plays, but that Elizabethan theatre offered lots of examples of actors who were guilty of over-acting both verbally and physically. In the original version, the actor playing Hamlet might have had some fun imitating other famous bad actors of the day, which would have amused the audience who might recognize his portrayals. The key to good acting comes in Hamlet's line, "the purpose of playing, whose end, both at the first, and now, was and is, to hold as 'twere the mirror up to nature."

Hamlet/Shakespeare also doesn't appreciate actors who play to the lowest level of the audience (the groundlings) or actors playing the clowns, or who adlib. I wonder if Shakespeare had an actor or two who did just that. He clearly had two comic actors of two different sizes: one for the Sir Toby Belch/Falstaff parts and the other for the Sir Andrew Aguecheek/Clown (*King Lear*) parts.

Once the players leave to get ready for the play, Polonius arrives with Rosencrantz and Guildenstern. The first thing Hamlet wants to know is whether the king is coming to the play. Once he is assured, he sends

Polonius and Rosencrantz and Guildenstern to speed up the actors.

Horatio arrives and Hamlet takes him into his confidence about the purpose of the play. He also tells Horatio how much he values his friendship He admires Horatio's ability to deal with life's ups and downs in a calm manner "for thou has been/As on, in suffering all, that suffers nothing,/A man that fortune's buffets and rewards/Hast ta'en with equal things:… Give me that man/ That is not passion's slave, and I will wear him/ In my heart's core, ay, in my heart of heart,/ As I do thee." It's important for the audience to know why Horatio has earned Hamlet's trust, to know what he values in others, what, perhaps, he would like to be more like himself. Hamlet asks Horatio to watch Claudius carefully during the play and then they will compare their observations afterwards. Hamlet trusts Horatio to undertake this role. Hamlet is desperate to have the evidence he needs to revenge his father's death. And he wants it from a rational source.

This scene up until now has shown the audience a completely sane and rational Hamlet. As soon as the audience enters to watch the play, his manner changes. Whether it is simply a role he chooses to play or whether he behaves this way because of the pressure of what he is hoping for is for the actor and the director to decide—perhaps his behavior is because of a combination of the two.

Hamlet's exchanges with Ophelia are basically rude and insulting. She keeps her composure well under the circumstances. Polonius would no doubt be listening to every word.

It's clear that for a part of the scene where the actors enact the mime show and even part of the actual play that Claudius is not paying much attention. And Gertrude doesn't seem to notice the action of the mime show being relevant either. We know that she does start to pay attention to the play before Claudius does from her answer to Hamlet's question about whether she is enjoying the play. She is focused on the character of the queen and says, "The lady doth protest too much, methinks." Worth remembering here that the Ghost accused Gertrude of adultery.

Claudius seems to start focusing now and asks what the name of the play is. The title, *The Mousetrap*, is Hamlet's invention, as earlier it was referred to as the *Murder of Gonzago*. When the actual murder is enacted by the players, Claudius reacts and stands. Once the king stands, everyone else has to do the same, so the scene starts to become unsettled. Claudius calls for lights and exits with the rest of the court leaving Hamlet and Horatio alone. Hamlet is thrilled that his plan has worked, and his behavior borders on the hysterical. Horatio does confirm that he saw the same reaction from Claudius that Hamlet saw.

Rosencrantz and Guildenstern enter confirming that Claudius is "Marvellous distemper'd ... with choler (anger.) and they tell Hamlet that Gertrude is upset and wants to speak with him. Guildenstern doesn't get the clear answer he wants to hear to the Queen's request, and Hamlet replies that he can't give him the "Wholesome" answer that he wants because he is mad (wit's diseas'd).

Hamlet knows that Rosencrantz and Guildenstern will report everything back to Claudius, so he tells them that the reason for his madness is thwarted ambition. It would have been natural for him to expect to inherit the throne after his father's death.

He can't resist showing his feelings for Rosencrantz and Guildenstern and letting them know that he knows about their spying when he talks about the recorder and how they are trying to control him to make him say what they want him to say like a musician makes a tune play on a recorder. He makes fun of Polonius before he goes, too.

When Hamlet is alone at the end of the scene he comments on the hour "the witching time of night,/when churchyards yawn." This foreshadows the next appearance of the ghost and Polonius' murder as well, when he says he could "drink hot blood, And do such bitter business as the day/Would quake to look on."

Questions

1. Why does Hamlet want Horatio to watch Claudius during the play?
2. Considering that the ghost has told Hamlet that Gertrude committed adultery, what is ironic about her line saying that she thinks the queen in the play "doth protest too much."
3. What is Claudius' reaction when he sees his murder acted out?
4. Explain why you think Hamlet is now sure that Claudius killed his father.
5. What do Rosencrantz and Guildenstern ask Hamlet to do when the play is over?

Scene 3

Claudius doesn't pray. Hamlet doesn't kill him.

At the beginning of this scene, Claudius is getting his report from Rosencrantz and Guildenstern. He advises them that he is sending them to England with Hamlet because he is afraid that Hamlet is after his throne. "/the terms of our estate may not endure/Hazard so near us...."

Rosencrantz and Guildenstern make flattering speeches about the power of kings and how their subjects depend on them. Polonius tells Claudius that

Hamlet has agreed to see Gertrude and that he is going to watch the meeting and report to Claudius later.

Left alone, Claudius attempts to pray and ask forgiveness for his sins, and the audience hears him admit to the murder of his brother. His line about the amount of blood on his hands echoes that of Macbeth. They both believe that there isn't enough water to wash the blood away. As he tries to pray, he can't find the words. He doesn't see how he can ask forgiveness when he doesn't want to give up what he gained from the sin he committed. As he tries again to pray, Hamlet enters and sees him defenseless.

Hamlet thinks he has found the perfect opportunity to murder Claudius while no one is around, but then he thinks that if he kills him while he's praying he might send Claudius to heaven, something that was denied his father because he was murdered without having confessed his sins. He decides to wait for a better time to kill Claudius that will ensure that he goes to hell. He leaves to go see is mother.

Of course, the irony is that Claudius wasn't praying anyway, and that Hamlet could have murdered him and achieved his purpose. "My words fly up, my thoughts remain below: / Words without thoughts never to heaven go."

Questions

1. Where is Hamlet going to be sent? Why is Claudius sending him there?
2. What do we learn about Claudius while he is praying?
3. Why doesn't Hamlet kill Claudius when he is alone with him? What is ironic about his decision to not kill Claudius?

Scene 4

Hamlet visits his mother and Polonius is killed.

The scene opens with Polonius hiding behind a curtain at the side of the room after giving Gertrude advice about what to say to Hamlet.

The verbal sparring begins almost as soon as Hamlet enters the room with the exchange of their first few lines. It's clear that he has no intention of being scolded by his mother for his behavior and turns her words against her right away. "Hamlet, thou has thy father much offended." "Mother, you have my father much offended." "Come, come, you answer with an idle tongue." "Go, go, thou question with a wicked tongue."

As he forces her to sit and listen to him, she asks, "What wilt thou do? Thou wilt not murder me? / Help, ho!" Polonius takes up the cry for help, and Hamlet, thinking it is Claudius attacks the person behind the curtain with his sword and kills him. Just before he finds out the identity of the body, he accuses his mother of being a part of the murder plot "almost as bad, good mother, / As kill a king, and marry with his brother."

She seems genuinely surprised by the comment "kill a king" which we might interpret as her not knowing about the murder, yet I think it's fair to assume that she does love Claudius and was likely having an affair with him before her husband died. Hamlet's words about Polonius are less than flattering.

Finally, Hamlet faces Gertrude with what he believes is her sin of incest and of lust for Claudius who is so clearly a lesser man compared to Hamlet's father. Claudius is described as diseased "mildew'd" and he described the relationship between Gertrude and Claudius as "to live/In the rank and sweat of an enseamed bed,/Stewe'd in corruption," Gertude asks him to stop accusing her and finally the Ghost appears to tell him to take care of Gertrude and help her deal with the news that Hamlet has just told her.

Gertrude can neither see nor hear the Ghost and thinks Hamlet must truly be mad. A good question for the class to debate is why the Ghost chose not to be visible to Gertrude, when he was visible to the guards and Horatio.

Hamlet is afraid that because Gertrude thinks he is mad that she will ignore his advice and he encourages her to confess what is past and avoid further contact with Claudius. "Lay not that flattering unction to your soul, / That not your trespass but my madness speaks. / …Confess yourself to heaven, / Repent what's past, avoid what is to come" This speech is full of references to corruption, disease and rot.

Hamlet is sorry to have murdered Polonius because the murder puts him in control of others, like Claudius who must find a way to get justice for Polonius' family and the court. He reassures Gertrude that he is not mad and she replies that she will do as he asks. They talk of his going to England, and Hamlet reveals that he has plans to get revenge on Rosencrantz and Guildenstern for their conniving on Claudius' behalf. "For 'tis the sport to have the engineer / Hoist with his own petard, and 't shall go hard / But I will delve one yard below their mines, / And blow them to the moon." Gertrude keeps up the pretense that Hamlet is mad.

Questions

1. After reading this scene, do you think Gertrude knew that Claudius killed her husband? Explain your answer.
2. Describe Hamlet's reaction when he realizes he has killed Polonius.
3. What instructions does Hamlet give Gertrude at the end of the scene?
4. Gertrude tells Hamlet that he will be going to England. What plans does he have for Rosencrantz and Guildenstern.

Act 4

Scene 1

Claudius has a plan.

Gertrude enters in a high state of emotion and tells Claudius and Rosencrantz and Guildenstern that Hamlet has killed Polonius and taken the body away. Claudius' first thought is how he escaped being murdered himself, and then he considers how he can keep this contained—a true politician. He can use Hamlet's madness as an excuse for the murder. He calls Rosencrantz and Guildenstern to go find Hamlet and bring Polonius' body to the chapel.

Questions

1. How does Claudius react to the news that Hamlet has killed Polonius?
2. What is his first priority?

Scene 2

R&G don't get an answer.

R&G ask Hamlet where he has hidden Polonius' body. He insults them by saying they are sponges and then tells them to take him to the king.

Scene 3

Claudius worries, gets insulted, and plots.

Claudius enters worrying about how to handle the consequences of what Hamlet has done. Hamlet is well liked so Claudius has to make the right decision or the people might turn against him.

When Hamlet answers, Claudius asks him where Polonius is hidden. Hamlet replies using his wit to annoy and insult Claudius. He tells him to send someone to look for Polonius in heaven and if he's not there Claudius himself should look for him in the other place—essentially telling Claudius to go to hell or, at the least, that hell is where he will be going eventually. Once Hamlet admits that Polonius is hidden under the stairs, Claudius tells him that he is leaving for England that night and he hurries Hamlet away to board the ship as soon as possible. Once alone, Claudius reveals that he is sending a letter to the king of England telling him to kill Hamlet. England pays homage to Denmark at this time, so he is sure England will do as he asks.

Questions

1. Why does Claudius worry about the decisions he needs to make about what to do with Hamlet?
2. What is he asking the king of England to do? Why is he sure that the king will do as he asks?

Scene 4

Fortinbras arrives. Hamlet vows to change his ways

Fortinbras asks a captain to go to the Danish court to ask for an escort across Denmark to Poland where he is going to reclaim land that belongs to Norway. Fortinbras exits and Hamlet asks the captain about Fortinbras and the cause that he is fighting for. The captain explains that the piece of land in dispute is small and practically worthless, but two countries will kill many men over it.

Alone, Hamlet compares Fortinbras' quest with his own. He has more reason to fight his battle than Fortinbras has to fight his, and yet Hamlet has done nothing. He is angry at himself for his delay and declares to stop procrastinating: "O from this time forth / My thoughts be bloody or nothing worth!"

Questions

1. Compare Hamlet and Fortinbras.
2. What decision does Hamlet make at the end of his soliloquy?

Scene 5

Ophelia is mad. Laertes is angry.

A gentleman, Horatio, and Gertrude discuss Ophelia's madness. Gertrude doesn't want to see her but is encouraged to do so. Ophelia enters singing songs of death and love. Claudius sees her distracted state and knows its cause. After Ophelia leaves, Claudius recaps the action, explaining that the kingdom is restless because of the poor funeral they gave Polonius, the news of Ophelia's madness, and the return of Laertes whom many people are joining against Claudius.

A messenger comes in with the news that Laertes and his mob are entering the castle and yelling that Laertes should be king. Laertes and the mob burst into the room. Laertes sends them away so he can speak to Claudius. Gertrude tries to protect Claudius while Claudius tells Laertes that he will explain everything that happened and then Laertes will know that he was not to blame.

Ophelia enters and Laertes realizes what has happened to her. Once she leaves, Claudius offers to meet with Laertes and a few of his trusted men, and he will explain what happened and the men can decide his fate.

Questions

1. What has happened to Ophelia?
2. What is Claudius worried about?
3. How does Claudius manage to calm Laertes?
4. What is Laertes' reaction to Ophelia's madness?

Scene 6

Horatio reads a letter.

Horatio receives a letter from Hamlet describing his escape on a pirate ship. He says he will meet Horatio soon.

Questions

1. What do we learn about Hamlet from the letter he has sent Horatio?
2. How do you think Hamlet's return will affect the plot?

Scene 7

Claudius and Laertes plot Hamlet's death. Ophelia drowns.

Claudius and Laertes have reconciled. Claudius explains that between Gertrude's love of Hamlet and the citizens' of Denmark's regard for him, that he could not sentence Hamlet to death. Messengers come with news that Hamlet is back in Denmark and will be arriving the next day. Laertes is eager to get his revenge, but Claudius has a plan that will allow Laertes to kill Hamlet, but also ensure that the death will be considered an accident, which will pacify the people and Gertrude.

Claudius is going to arrange a friendly duel between Laertes and Hamlet. Laertes will use a sword that has not been blunted and to make sure that he kills Hamlet, Laertes will put poison on the sword point. Claudius will prepare a goblet for Hamlet to drink from when he is thirsty from fighting and put poison in it, too.

Gertrude enters with news of Ophelia's death by drowning.

Questions

1. What is Claudius' plan to have Hamlet killed? What is Laertes planning to do to

make sure that Hamlet dies? How does Claudius plan to help?

2. Describe what happens to Ophelia.

ACT 5

Scene 1

Graves, grave diggers, philosophy, and a funeral

The scene opens with a conversation between a gravedigger and his friend about the person for whom they are preparing the grave. It's Ophelia's grave and the two men debate how she could have a Christian burial if she committed suicide. Though the verdict was given by the coroner, the men believe that she will be buried in consecrated ground because she is a gentlewoman—a person of status.

Hamlet and Horatio enter and watch the gravedigger for a while and comment on how cheerful he is about his job. Hamlet finds skulls and muses on the transience of life. He asks the gravedigger whom the grave is being dug for and there is much wordplay that includes comments about Hamlet, as well. While talking about how long it takes a corpse to rot, Hamlet finds a skull and asks whose it is. It is his old court jester, Yorick. Hamlet tells Horatio about Yorick.

When they see the court coming to the graveyard, they hide to watch. When Hamlet realizes that the grave belongs to Ophelia he rushes forward, and he and Laertes quarrel at the grave about who loved Ophelia more.

Hamlet rushes off followed by Horatio, and Claudius reminds Laertes that he will have his revenge and to be patient.

Questions

1. What hints are we given that the grave is being dug is for Ophelia?
2. What do Hamlet and Laertes quarrel about at Ophelia's grave?

Scene 2

Hamlet arranges the deaths of Rosencrantz and Guildenstern. Hamlet and Laertes duel. Hamlet, Laertes, Gertrude and Claudius die.

At the beginning of the scene, Hamlet describes his escape to Horatio. He explains how he changed the letter ordering his death to ordering the deaths of Rosencrantz and Guildenstern. Osric arrives with news of the proposed duel. Hamlet's wit and humor are evident as he and Horatio make fun of Osric.

Before the duel, Hamlet makes an attempt to reconcile with Laertes, explaining his madness and saying how sorry he is for what he has done. Laertes pretends to accept the apology and they choose their weapons. Claudius shows off a pearl that he will put in the cup for the winner of the first hit.

They duel, and Laertes is struck first. Claudius puts the pearl into the wine and encourages Hamlet to drink, but he says not yet. After he scores another hit, he still does not drink, so Gertrude toasts him with the poisoned wine. Claudius makes a small attempt to stop her, but he can't without giving himself away.

They fight again and Laertes wounds Hamlet. In the scuffle, they exchange swords and Hamlet wounds Laertes. Gertrude is unwell and Horatio sees that both men are bleeding. Gertrude begins to swoon, and when Claudius blames it on the sight of the blood, she says she has been poisoned by the wine. Hamlet yells for the room to be closed off.

Laertes confesses to poisoning the sword, and confirms that Gertrude is poisoned and that Claudius is to blame. Hamlet wounds the king with the poisoned sword, too, and then forces him to drink the rest of the poisoned wine. Claudius dies followed by Laertes.

Hamlet asks Horatio to explain everything that has happened so that people will understand and not blame Hamlet. Horatio doesn't want to and wants to commit suicide instead. Hamlet persuades him to stay alive and tell his story. They hear gunfire and Osric reports that Fortinbras has arrived from Poland.

Hamlet hopes that Fortinbras will become the new king and once again asks Horatio to tell the story so that the new king will know the truth.

Fortinbras enters and is shocked at the sight of so many deaths. The ambassador from England reports that Rosencrantz and Guildenstern are dead, too. Horatio promises to explain everything to Fortinbras. Fortinbras commands captains to give Hamlet all the honors of a soldier and a king and orders the room cleared of the bodies. He shows he is very much in command and ready to be king. "Such a sight as this / Becomes the field but here shows much amiss. / Go, bid the soldiers shoot."

Questions

1. How has Hamlet arranged for the deaths of Rosencrantz and Guildenstern? Do you think that this action is justified? Explain your answer.
2. Before the duel, how does Hamlet attempt to make peace with Laertes?
3. What happens to the wine after it is poisoned by Claudius?
4. How does Hamlet end up poisoning Laertes?
5. How does Hamlet make sure that Claudius dies?

6. What does Hamlet want Horatio to do after Hamlet's death?

CHAPTER 6

Journal Prompts for *Hamlet*

Here are some ideas for journal prompts for *Hamlet*, including some ideas for writing the missing soliloquies in the play.

1. Do you agree with Hamlet that some people are just born corrupt or evil? Give reasons for your answer.

2. Do you believe in ghosts? Why or why not?

3. How would you feel if your parents told you to stop seeing your boyfriend or girlfriend? What would you do?

4. What advice would you give to someone who was leaving home to go to school or work?

5. How can you tell if your friends are being honest with you?

6. How would you feel if you found out that a friend was talking about you behind your back or was reporting what you did to your parents?

7. What does Ophelia write in her diary the night her father is killed by Hamlet?

8. Why do you think Gertrude can't see her husband's ghost and Hamlet, Horatio and the guards can?

9. Write Hamlet's letter to Ophelia when he's on the ship to England apologizing for the death of Polonius.

10. Hamlet doesn't like bad actors. Which actor/actress do you think is overrated and why?

11. Here are some suggestions for some missing soliloquies in the play. What would these characters say in these situations?
    a. Ophelia after Polonius tells her to avoid Hamlet
    b. Ophelia after she learns about the death of her father
    c. Laertes after he and Claudius agree to kill Hamlet

d. Gertrude after Hamlet returns during Ophelia's funeral
e. Claudius before the duel

CHAPTER 7

The *Hamlet* Essay

Topics

Here are a few five-paragraph essay topics that you can use for summative evaluation or put on an exam.

Discuss Hamlet *as a tragic hero.*
Possible talking points:
Tragic hero is a person of noble birth//Hamlet is Prince of Denmark
Tragic hero makes a decision that affects his downfall//Hamlet agrees to avenge his father's murder
Hero has a tragic flaw//Hamlet's indecision
Hero's flaw influences his decision//Hamlet's delay in getting revenge results in his near madness, the loss of Ophelia's love, and many deaths
Hero's decision affects others//his decision to pretend to be mad while he waits to get revenge affects Ophelia who is forced to confront him by her father, and also Claudius and Gertrude who call for

Rosencrantz and Guildenstern to come and spy on Hamlet.

Deaths occur because of the hero//Polonius, Ophelia, Claudius, Laertes, Gertrude

The hero pays for his decision with his death//Hamlet dies

After the hero's death, order is restored//Fortinbras becomes king

Explain how the theme of Natural Order is used in the play.

Possible talking points:

The theme is used to define character.

a) Because Hamlet did not become king (the proper succession), his grief and anger at his mother and uncle overwhelm him.

b) Because Claudius has killed a king, he feels threatened, frightened, and cannot pray

The theme is used to instigate the action of the play

Because King Hamlet was murdered, his ghost walks and Denmark is threatened with war "something is rotten in the state of Denmark."

When Fortinbras becomes king at the end of the play, the audience leaves satisfied because the disruption to the natural order has been resolved a king taking the throne who has been chosen by Hamlet.

Discuss how the theme of corruption and disease is used in the play.

Possible talking points:

Hamlet describes his world as "an unweeded garden, / that grows to seed; things rank and gross in nature/ Possess it merely.

Act 1 scene4, Hamlet's speech: "So oft it changes in particular men, / That for some vicious more of nature in them, / … take corruption from that particular fault …."

Marcellus "Something is rotten in the state of Denmark." 1,4,90

Claudius: 3,3 "Oh, my offence is rank, it smells to heaven"

Hamlet: 3,3 "This physic but prolongs they sickly days."

Ophelia's madness

Other topics:

The roles of Ophelia and Gertrude in the play
Revenge—comparing Fortinbras, Laertes, and Hamlet
Loyalty and friendship
Filial Duty

Essay Organizer

To get a PDF of this organizer to hand out to your students, please go to this link. The following is a very pedestrian example of how the organizer works, but it should give you an idea of how your students can use the organizer to prepare their essays.

PARAGRAPH 1

Introduction: A general opening statement, for example: Shakespeare's play, *Hamlet*, is still being performed for audiences today, hundreds of years after it was originally written. One of the reasons that the play is so compelling is because of the audience's fascination with the character of Hamlet.

Thesis: **Hamlet is a tragic hero**, based on Aristotle's definition and showing characteristics that the audience can understand because he has flaws that the audience can relate to.

Statement of Direction: Hamlet is a tragic hero according to Aristotle's definition because he is a noble person who falls from power, he has a tragic flaw, and Hamlet's decision affects those around him with deadly consequences.

PARAGRAPH 2

Introduction tying argument to statement of direction

Hamlet is a noble person
Supporting Details
He is the Prince of Denmark. Quotes in which he is described in noble terms by Claudius, Ophelia, Horatio
Summary relating proofs to thesis
Because Hamlet is a noble person, he has an important characteristic of a tragic hero.

PARAGRAPH 3
Introduction tying argument to statement of direction
Hamlet has a tragic flaw
Supporting details
Examples from text of Hamlet's flaw which could be his tendency to think too much before he acts to revenge his father's death. Delaying tactics include feigning madness, setting up the play, not killing Claudius while he's praying. Quote his final statement after seeing Fortinbras and his army, "My thoughts be bloody …."
Summary relating proofs to thesis
Because of his flaw, Hamlet is a tragic hero.

PARAGRAPH 4
Introduction tying argument to statement of direction
Hamlet's decision affects those around him
Supporting Details

His decision to delay getting revenge for his father's death causes Ophelia to be used to trick him, ending their relationship, and probably being a first step to her madness. Because he doesn't kill Claudius right away, Claudius has time to bring in spies (Rosencrantz and Guildenstern) and plot to have him taken to England. His decision not to act until he is sure Claudius is guilty sets up the play that leads to his rash behavior and forces a confrontation with his mother. That, in turn, leads to Polonius's death, his own exile, Ophelia's death, Laertes' need for revenge (leading leads him to be influenced by Claudius), and the resulting deaths in the final scene of the play..

Summary relating proofs to thesis

Because Hamlet's decision caused many other deaths, he is a tragic hero.

PARAGRAPH 5

Recap of Thesis

Hamlet shares many characteristics of the tragic hero.

Recap of Proofs

Hamlet was of noble birth and had a tragic flaw. His delay and indecision resulted in the deaths of many other including himself.

Summative statement

Since people continue to see news stories about heroes or celebrities whom they have held in high esteem who have hurt others due to a flaw in their characters, it's no wonder that Shakespeare's depiction of Hamlet as a tragic hero still resonates with audiences today.

Essay Evaluation

Here is a list of links for rubrics for essay evaluation. Choose the one that works best for you and for the expectations of your department administrators.

1. A great how-to for creating rubrics with examples for essay evaluation

http://www.nuigalway.ie/celt/teaching_and_learning/Rubrics_QG_v1.1.2.pdf

2. For ESL learners

http://www.wcs.k12.va.us/users/honaker/Rubric4c-Writing-rubric.pdf

3. From NCTE

http://www.readwritethink.org/files/resources/printouts/Essay%20Rubric.pdf

4. For Grade 8s

This is a Word document, so it could be changed to match your grade level. It's very comprehensive

https://www.google.ca/url?sa=t&rct=j&q=&esrc=s&source=web&cd=8&ved=0CDgQFjAH&url=http%3A%2F%2Ffhenglishlab.wikispaces.com%2Ffile%2Fview%2FEssay%2BEvaluation%2BRubric.doc&ei=03jLVNHkEMKPyASMmoGYDg&usg=AFQjCNHNy-

_KXtHYSZt660p_nshJWWrzBg&sig2=GMXd0E5NW
pURGjD-wDqswQ&cad=rja

5. Another Word document that you can adapt
https://www.google.ca/url?sa=t&rct=j&q=&esrc=s&
source=web&cd=16&ved=0CDsQFjAFOAo&url=https
%3A%2F%2Fonlineteachingandlearning.wikispaces.co
m%2Ffile%2Fview%2FRubric%2Bfor%2BGrading%2
Band%2BEvaluating%2BEssays.doc&ei=eXrLVM6-
F4WiyATg54HYCg&usg=AFQjCNFxkyKnOdJ_85HE
OrrIFr8xuYK4UQ&sig2=F_0ewxRMBjJOUx6WveTd
0w&cad=rja

CHAPTER 8

Online Resources

Rather than reinvent the wheel, here is a list of links you can use to find tests, homework questions, essays, projects, class activities, etc. for *Hamlet*. Links to Cliff Notes and Spark Notes are included because, after all, you may as well know what your students are reading.

1) ***Hamlet* Study Guide at Shakespeare Online:**
   http://www.shakespeare-online.com/plays/hamlet/hamletresources.html
- the site features synopses, analysis, study quiz (with detailed answers), comparisons between plays, essay topics, and a discussion of Shakespearean and Elizabethan Tragedy

2) **Teaching *Hamlet,* Resources from Folger Education:**
   http://www.folger.edu/template.cfm?cid=2782&CFID=69108994&CFTOKEN=76589575 – contains teaching modules, lesson plans, notes, links to videos and podcasts, as well as curricula on performance-based teaching

3) *Hamlet*, **from the Royal Shakespeare Company:**
http://www.rsc.org.uk/education/resources/bank/hamlet/teacher-packs/ - contains a teacher pack based on exploration of themes and relationships in the play

4) *Hamlet* **Lesson Plans and Other Teaching Resources at Web English Teacher:**
http://www.webenglishteacher.com/hamlet.html - contains a collection of lessons plans and teachers' guides, as well as activities, relating to teaching *Macbeth*.

5) *Hamlet* **on Cliffnotes:**
http://www.cliffsnotes.com/literature/h/hamlet/hamlet-at-a-glance -features summaries and analysis for every scene, major characters, quizzes, essay questions and practices projects

6) *Hamlet:* **Study Questions from California Polytechnic:**
http://cla.calpoly.edu/~dschwart/engl339/hamlet.html - a collection of in-depth questions examining themes, characters, and links to resources on tragedy and revenge tragedy. Recommended for advanced students, such as AP or IB.

7) *Hamlet* **at Shakespeare*Help*.com:**
http://www.shakespearehelp.com/hamlet.htm - contains many study and teaching guides for Shakespeare, from links to websites, essays,

articles on individual study topics, as well as lesson plans, and free quizzes for Act 1 – paid services also available

8) *Hamlet* **on Sparknotes:** http://www.sparknotes.com/shakespeare/hamlet - contains general info, analysis and plot overviews, as well as act analyses, a quiz, and study questions and essay topics

9) *This is Hamlet* **in the Classroom:** http://thisishamlet.com/bm.assets/PDF/ThisIsHamlet_LessonPlans.pdf f - collection of lesson plans and resources for teachers of *Macbeth,* based on the DVD but contains useful activities

10) **Shakespeare Resource Center:** http://www.bardweb.net/plays/index.html - contains synopses of all Shakespeare plays, as well as links to further resources on each play

ABOUT THE AUTHOR

Heather Wright is a former middle and high school English teacher, currently teaching business communications at her local college. Her website, http://wrightingwords.com provides inspiration and tips for teen and pre-teen writers and their teachers. She is also a freelance writer who has been published in local, national and international publications. She often works for publishers preparing teacher support material for textbooks.

Printed in Great Britain
by Amazon.co.uk, Ltd.,
Marston Gate.